the Word Revealed

*A festival service to commemorate the
400th anniversary of the King James Bible*

*compiled by
Peter Moger and Charles Taylor*

The Royal School of Church Music
19 The Close, Salisbury, Wiltshire, SP1 2EB, England
Tel: +44 (0)1722 424848 Fax: +44 (0)1722 424849
Email: press@rscm.com Website: www.rscm.com
Registered charity 312828

the Word Revealed

Texts of the introduction, commentaries, music and graphic images are
copyright © 2010 The Royal School of Church Music,
except where otherwise attributed.

Some material is taken from Common Worship: Services and Prayers
for the Church of England,
© 2000–2010 the Archbishops' Council, and is used with permission.

RSCM Catalogue Number: RS40
ISBN: 978-0-85402-184-0

Cover design by Anthony Marks
Music and text origination by RSCM Press and MusicLines
Cover picture: John's Gospel Chapter 1 from the King James Bible
with thanks to the American Bible Society
Dedication page in The Holy Bible, publ. by Robert Barker, 1611, English School, (17th century)
Frontispiece to The Holy Bible, publ. by Robert Barker, 1611, Cornelis Boel, (c.1576–1621)
Private Collection / The Bridgeman Art Library

Printed in Great Britain by Halstan Group Ltd

Contents

Introduction

The year 2011 marks the 400th anniversary of the King James Bible which, in the words of the Archbishop of Canterbury, 'remains a unique monument of scholarship, devotion and imagination, [and] which has a crucial place in our common life.' *The Word Revealed* aims to set the King James Bible within an historical and liturgical context – tracing the story of the Bible in the English language, and linking this to the wider issue of the place held by Holy Scripture within the life and worship of the Church.

The Bible has always been at the heart of Christian life, worship and mission. From earliest times, the ordered reading of Holy Scripture has taken place within gatherings for worship. A large proportion of Christian liturgy and song in both the Catholic and Reformed traditions is derived directly from the words of Scripture and, in the churches which owe their genesis to the Reformation, confessional statements and articles of belief point to the centrality of the Bible.

A helpful summary of the place of Scripture in the life of the Churches of the Anglican tradition is given in the Collect for the Second Sunday in Advent (often called 'Bible Sunday') in the Book of Common Prayer. Here, we are reminded that Scripture was written in order to teach God's people, that Christians need to engage with it ('hear, read, mark, learn and inwardly digest [it]') in order to 'embrace and ever hold fast' the hope of everlasting life in Christ.

The 1611 King James Bible (or 'Authorized Version') may be seen as a crucial landmark within a process of English Bible translation which stretches from the late Middle Ages until the present day. In the past 400 years, the influence of the King James Bible has been felt in ways too numerous to list, both within and outside the Church: on worship, on literature and on the English language itself. It is still read regularly in Christian worship and, even where it is not, many of its cadences remain through those translations which have sought to maintain resonances with the King James Bible.

The Service

The Word Revealed has been designed within the parameters of A Service of the Word – a flexible structure in which the reading of Scripture is juxtaposed with praise, reflection and prayer. An opening 'Gathering' and final 'Sending' section frame a central core of 'Recalling and Reflecting', in which the story of the Bible in English is told in five episodes. In each episode, a spoken introduction sets an historical context and is followed by a Scripture reading, musical items and a specific liturgical action. A range of musical resources has been provided for use within the given structure. This includes hymns, songs and choral anthems of varying degrees of difficulty.

Care should be taken over the ordering of space for this act of worship. As befits a celebration of Holy Scripture, the lectern (or the place from which the Bible is read) should be prominent within the worship space. If candles are to be used, as is suggested for the 'light prayer' in the Gathering (pages 3–5), they should be of sufficient size as to make them visible throughout the building. Likewise, the copies of the Gospels, Bible and Book of Common Prayer should be large and should be placed prominently.

The fourth reflection ('Into all the World') includes the reading of the account of the Great Commission and a Thanksgiving for Baptism. This should take place, wherever possible, at the normal place of baptism within the building which, in many churches will be an historic font. If, however, there are issues of access and visibility, an alternative 'station' might be considered, perhaps towards the rear of the Nave, with a large bowl being placed centrally on a stand. What is important is that, if at all possible, this part of the service take place in a location other than that of the 'regular' reading of Scripture, thus suggesting the 'outward movement' which flows from the Gospel imperative to 'make disciples of all nations.'

Several translations and one paraphrase version of the Bible have been used in the service, ranging from the Greek text of verses from St John's Gospel, through Tyndale and Coverdale's translations, to the King James Version of 1611, the New Revised Standard Version and The Message. Readers are encouraged to use the specified versions where possible, but modern language alternatives have been provided for the Greek and Tyndale texts.

Peter Moger
Precentor, York Minster

Charles Taylor
Dean of Peterborough Cathedral

Using the book

This book provides both a framework for a service and a repertory of texts and music. It can be used in the form in which it is presented in Part I (pages 1–57), with choral items selected from Part II (pages 59–115), or by substituting other musical settings or texts appropriate to the context of the worship. Where music is offered in Part II, page references are indicated in the main text.

Performance notes are available on the RSCM website, www.rscm.com, where you can also find a text for the preparation of a congregational service leaflet.

Outline of the Service

The Gathering

I – The Early Church

II – A Bible in Every Church

III – Appointed to be Read in Churches

IV – Into all the World

V – According to the Latest Translation

The Sending Out

the Word Revealed

PART I: THE SERVICE

TO THE MOST
HIGH AND MIGHTIE

Prince, I A M E S by the grace of God
King of Great Britaine, France and Ireland,
Defender of the Faith, &c.

THE TRANSLATORS OF *THE BIBLE*,
wish Grace, Mercie, and Peace, through I E S V S
CHRIST *our* LORD.

G Reat and manifold were the blessings (most dread
Soueraigne) which Almighty G o D, the Father
of all Mercies, bestowed vpon vs the people of
E N G L A N D, when first he sent your Maiesties
Royall person to rule and raigne ouer vs. For
whereas it was the expectation of many, who
wished not well vnto our S I o N, that vpon the
setting of that bright *Occidentall Starre* Queene
E L I Z A B E T H of most happy memory, some
thicke and palpable cloudes of darkenesse would so haue ouershadowed
this land, that men should haue bene in doubt which way they were to
walke, and that it should hardly be knowen, who was to direct the vnsetled
State: the appearance of your M A I E S T I E, as of the *Sunne* in his strength,
instantly dispelled those supposed and surmised mists, and gaue vnto all
that were well affected, exceeding cause of comfort; especially when we beheld the gouernment established in your H I G H N E S S E, and your hope-
full Seed, by an vndoubted Title, and this also accompanied with Peace
and tranquillitie, at home and abroad.

But amongst all our Ioyes, there was no one that more filled our hearts,
then the blessed continuance of the Preaching of G o D s sacred word a-
mongst vs, which is that inestimable treasure, which excelleth all the riches
of the earth, because the fruit thereof extendeth it selfe, not onely to the time
spent in this transitory world, but directeth and disposeth men vr to that
Eternall happinesse which is aboue in Heauen.

Then, not to suffer this to fall to the ground, but rather to take it vp, and
to continue it in that state, wherein the famous predecessour of your H I G H-
N E S S E did leaue it; Nay, to goe forward with the confidence and reso-
lution

A 2

¶ The Gathering

A reader declaims

To the most high and mighty prince, James, the Translators of the Bible wish Grace, Mercy, and Peace, through Jesus Christ our Lord.

When Your Highness had once, out of deep judgment, apprehended how convenient it was, that, out of the Original sacred Tongues, there should be one more exact translation of the Holy Scriptures into the English Tongue; Your Majesty did never desist to urge and to excite those to whom it was commended, that the Work might be hastened, and that the business might be expedited in so decent a manner, as a matter of such importance might justly require.

And now at last, by the mercy of God, and the continuance of our labours, it being brought unto such a conclusion, as that we have great hopes that the Church of England shall reap good fruit thereby.

Adapted from the Preface to the Authorized Version 1611

And so may the grace, mercy and peace of Jesus Christ be with you all
All   **and also with you.**

During the following prayer, candles may be lit at the Lectern

Blessed are you, Sovereign God,
creator of light and darkness,
to you be glory and praise for ever.
As we gather, you renew your promise
to reveal among us the light of your presence.
May your word be a lantern to our feet
and a light upon our path
that we may behold your coming among us.
Strengthen us in our stumbling weakness
and free our tongues to sing your praise.
Blessed be God, Father, Son and Holy Spirit.
All   **Blessed be God for ever.**

Hymn: Thanks to God whose Word was spoken

ST HELEN

87 87 87

1 Thanks to God whose word was spoken
in the deed that made the earth.
His the voice that called a nation;
his the fires that tried her worth.
God has spoken, God has spoken:
praise God for his open word.

2 Thanks to God whose Word incarnate
heights and depths of life did share.
Deeds and words and death and rising,
grace in human form declare.
God has spoken, God has spoken:
praise God for his open word.

3 Thanks to God whose word was written
in the Bible's sacred page,
record of the revelation
showing God to every age.
God has spoken, God has spoken:
praise God for his open word.

4 Thanks to God whose word is published
in the tongues of every race.
See its glory undiminished
by the change of time and place.
God has spoken, God has spoken:
praise God for his open word.

5 Thanks to God whose word is answered
by the Spirit's voice within.
Here we drink of joy unmeasured,
life redeemed from death and sin.
God is speaking, God is speaking:
praise God for his open word.

Words: Reginald Thomas Brooks (1918–1985)
Words © 1954, Renewed 1982 by Hope Publishing Company, Carol Stream, IL 60188, USA
All rights reserved. Used by permission
Music: George Clement Martin (1844–1916)

Remain standing

Collect

Let us pray.

Silence is kept.

Blessed Lord,
who hast caused all holy Scriptures to be written for our learning:
grant that we may in such wise hear them,
read, mark, learn and inwardly digest them,
that by patience and comfort of thy holy word,
we may embrace and ever hold fast
the blessed hope of everlasting life,
which thou hast given us in our Saviour Jesus Christ,
who liveth and reigneth with thee,
in the unity of the Holy Spirit,
one God, now and for ever.

All   Amen.

Collect of the Second Sunday in Advent (Bible Sunday),
The Book of Common Prayer

Sit

¶ RECALLING AND REFLECTING

I – The Early Church

The Story: The Formation of the Canon of Scripture

Reader 1   Our Bible is the product of thousands of years of oral tradition, inspired writings and prayerful reflection within the community of faith. It was not until the 4th century AD that its content was finally agreed by Councils of the Church.

Reader 2   Just as the worshipping community had a key role in the formation of the Bible, so the proclamation of Scripture is an essential part of the offering of Christian worship.

We read in the Acts of the Apostles, that Paul, and his companions

Reader 1   went into the synagogue and sat down. After the reading of the law and the prophets, the officials of the synagogue sent them a message, saying, 'Brothers, if you have any word of exhortation for the people, give it.' So Paul stood up and with a gesture began to speak. "You Israelites, and others who fear God, listen."

Acts 13.14b–16a

Reader 2   The early Christian writers were anxious that their letters were read publicly within the local church. Paul writes to Timothy:

Reader 1   Until I arrive, give attention to the public reading of scripture, to exhorting, to teaching.

1 Tim 4.13

Reader 2   His concern is that, in reading Scripture, people would

Let the word of Christ dwell in [them] richly.

Col 3.16

We hear now from St Luke's account of Jesus reading the Scriptures in the Synagogue at Nazareth.

Reading: Luke 4.16–21

Jesus came to Nazareth, where he had been brought up, he went to the synagogue on the Sabbath day, as was his custom. He stood up to read, and the scroll of the prophet Isaiah was given to him. He unrolled the scroll and found the place where it was written:

'The Spirit of the Lord is upon me,
because he has anointed me
to bring good news to the poor.
He has sent me to proclaim release to the captives
and recovery of sight to the blind,
to let the oppressed go free,
to proclaim the year of the Lord's favour.'

And he rolled up the scroll, gave it back to the attendant, and sat down. The eyes of all in the synagogue were fixed on him. Then he began to say to them, 'Today this scripture has been fulfilled in your hearing.'

Your word, O Lord, is a lantern to our feet
All   and a light upon our path.

Musical Reflection

either
O praise the Lord
by **Adrian Batten** (c.1591–1637) Page 60
or
Teach me, O Lord
by **Thomas Attwood** (1765–1838) Page 64
or
Teach us, good Lord
by **David Ogden** (b.1964) Page 70

Liturgical Action

John 1.1–3a, 5, 14 is read (in Greek) while a copy of the Gospels is placed centrally. A large candle may be lit beside it.

1Ἐν ἀρ.χῇ ἦν ὁ λό.γος, καὶ ὁ λό.γος ἦν πρὸς τὸν θε.όν, καὶ θε.ὸς ἦν.ὁ λό.γος.

Enn arke en ho logos, kai ho logos en pros ton theon, kai theos en ho logos.

1. In the beginning was the Word, and the Word was with God, and the Word was God.

2οὗ.τος ἦν ἐν ἀρ.χῇ πρὸς τὸν θε.όν.

Ou tos en enn arke pros ton theon.

2. The same was in the beginning with God.

3πάν.τα δι' αὐ.τοῦ ἐ.γέ.νε.το, καὶ χω.ρὶς αὐ.τοῦ ἐ.γέ.νε.το οὐ.δὲ ἕν ὃ γέ.γο.νεν

Panta di auton egeneto kai choris auton egeneto oude enn ho gegonen.

3. All things were made by him; and without him was not any thing made that was made.

5καὶ τὸ φῶς ἐν τῇ σκο.τί.ᾳ φαί.νει, καὶ ἡ σκο.τί.α αὐ.τὸ οὐ κα.τέ.λα.βεν.

Kai to phos enn te skotia phainei, kai he skotia auto ou katelassen.

5. And the light shineth in darkness; and the darkness comprehended it not.

14καὶ ὁ λό.γος σὰρξ ἐ.γέ.νε.το καὶ ἐσ.κή.νω.σεν ἐν ἡ.μῖν, καὶ ἐ.θε.α.σά.με.θα τὴν δόξ.αν αὐ.τοῦ, δόξ.αν ὡς μο.νο.γε.νοῦς πα.ρὰ πατ.ρός, πλή.ρης χά.ρι.τος καὶ ἀ.λη.θεί.ας.

Kai ho logos sarks egeneto kai eskenosen enn hemin kai etheasametha ten doxan autou, doxan hos monogenous para patros, pleres karitos kai aletheias.

14. And the Word was made flesh, and dwelt among us, (and we beheld his glory, the glory as of the only begotten of the Father,) full of grace and truth.

Collect

Let us pray.

Silence is kept.

O Lord God,
who art the source of all truth and love,
keep us faithful to the apostles' teaching and fellowship,
united in prayer,
and one in joy and simplicity of heart,
in Jesus Christ our Lord.

All   Amen.

Adapted from the Post Communion for the Fourteenth Sunday after Trinity (Common Worship)

Hymn: Teach us to love the scriptures, Lord

ST BOTOLPH

86 86 (CM)

1   Teach us to love the Scriptures, Lord,
       to read and mark and learn;
    and daily in your written word
       the living Word discern.

2   Your purposes in us fulfil
       as we your promise claim,
    who seek to know and do your will
       and learn to love your Name.

3   When in some dark and cloudy day
       beset by fears we stand,
    your word be light upon our way,
       a sword within our hand.

4   As on your word our spirits feed
       through all its pages shine;
    make known yourself to us who read,
       the Bread of life divine.

5   So shall the treasures of your word
       become as sacred ground;
    teach us to love the Scriptures, Lord,
       where Christ is surely found.

Words: Timothy Dudley-Smith (b.1926)
Copyright © Timothy Dudley-Smith in Europe and Africa;
© Hope Publishing Company for the United States of America and the rest of the world.
Reproduced by permission of Oxford University Press

Music: Gordon Slater (1896–1979)
© Oxford University Press, Great Clarendon Street, Oxford, OX2 6DP
Reproduced by permission. All rights reserved.

For alternative hymn: Lord, thy word abideth, please turn over

Hymn: Lord, thy word abideth

RAVENSHAW

66 66

1   Lord, thy word abideth,
    and our footsteps guideth;
    who its truth believeth
    light and joy receiveth.

2   When our foes are near us,
    then thy word doth cheer us,
    word of consolation,
    message of salvation.

3   When the storms are o'er us,
    and dark clouds before us,
    then its light directeth,
    and our way protecteth.

4   Who can tell the pleasure,
    who recount the treasure,
    by thy word imparted
    to the simple-hearted?

5   Word of mercy, giving
    succour to the living;
    word of life, supplying
    comfort to the dying!

6   O that we discerning
    its most holy learning,
    Lord, may love and fear thee,
    evermore be near thee.

Words: Henry Williams Baker (1821–1877)
Music: Mediæval German Melody
adapted and harmonised by William Henry Monk
(1823–1889)

II – A Bible in Every Church

The Story: The Bible in English

Reader 1   The pressure for reform, founded on Scripture, began long before the period we would associate with the Reformation. In the 14th century, John Wyclif was proclaiming the Bible as the only criterion of doctrine; and although he probably played no direct part in the translation of the Bible attributed to him, he inspired the work.

Reader 2   More significant was the work of William Tyndale, who conceived the project of translating the Bible into English in 1522, resulting in his exile to Germany. His first translation of the New Testament arrived in England in 1526, followed by parts of the Old Testament. Together, these formed the basis of the King James Bible of 1611, but they cost Tyndale his life. He was burned at the stake in 1536.

Reader 1   But it was too late to close the floodgates – already in 1534 Convocation had petitioned King Henry VIII that the whole Bible might be translated into English. In 1535 Miles Coverdale published a complete Bible dedicated to the King based on Tyndale's text. Coverdale's translation of the Book of Psalms was included in the Books of Common Prayer (1549–1662) and remains much-loved to this day.

Reader 2   In 1538 it was decreed that a copy of the Bible in English be placed in every church.

Liturgical Action

During the singing of verses from Psalm 119, a large bible is placed on the lectern.

Musical Reflection

Psalm 119.161–168

1 – Plainchant

161   Princes have persecuted *me* withˆout a cause :
     but my heart standeth in *awe* of thy word.

162   I am as *glad* of thy word :
     as one that find-*eth* great spoils.

163   As for lies, I hate *and* ab-hor them :
     but thy law *do* I love.

164   Seven times a day *do* I praise thee :
     because of thy right-*eous* judge-ments.

165   Great is the peace that they *have* whoˆlove thy law :
     and they are not offend-*ed* at it.

166   Lord, I have looked *for* thyˆsa-ving health :
     and done after thy *com*-mand-ments.

167   My soul hath kept thy *tes*-ti-mon-ies :
     and loved them *ex*-ceedˆing-ly.

168   I have kept thy commandments and *tes*-ti-mon-ies :
     for all my ways are *be*-fore thee.

Words: Psalm 119.161–168 in Coverdale's Psalter 1535
Music: Tone iii

II – Simple chant

161   Princes have persecuted me without a | cause :
         but my heart standeth in awe of thy | word.

162   I am as glad of thy | word :
         as one that findeth great | spoils.

163   As for lies, I hate and ab- | hor them :
         but thy law do I | love.

164   Seven times a day do I | praise thee :
         because of thy righteous | judgements.

165   Great is the peace that they have who love thy | law :
         and they are not offended | at it.

166   Lord, I have looked for thy saving | health :
         and done after thy com- | mandments.

167   My soul hath kept thy | testimonies :
         and loved them ex- | ceedingly.

168   I have kept thy commandments and | testimonies :
         for all my ways are be- | fore thee.

Words: Psalm 119.161–168 in Coverdale's Psalter 1535
Music © Peter Moger (b.1964)

Reading: Romans 15.4–13

A reading from the Letter to the Romans.

Whatsoever thinges are written afore tyme are written for oure learnynge
that we thorow pacience and comforte of the scripture myght have hope.
The God of pacience and consolacion geve vnto every one of you that ye be
lyke mynded one towardes another after the insample of Christ: that ye all
agreynge together maye with one mouth prayse God the father of oure Lorde
Iesus.

Wherfore receave ye one another as Christ receaved vs to the prayse of
God. And I saye that Iesus Christ was a minister of the circumcision for the
trueth of god to conferme the promyses made vnto the fathers. And let the
gentyls prayse god for his mercy as it is written:

> For this cause I will prayse the amonge the gentyls
> and synge in thy name.
> And agayne he sayth:
> reioyse ye gentyles with his people.
> And agayne
> prayse the Lorde all ye gentyls
> and laude him all nacions.
> And in another place Esaias sayth:
> ther shalbe the rote of Iesse
> and he that shall ryse ro raygne over the gentyls:
> in him shall the gentyls trust.

The God of hope fyll you with all ioye and peace in belevynge: that ye maye
be ryche in hope thorowe the power of the holy goost.

From William Tyndale's Bible (1522)

Whatever was written in former days was written for our instruction, so that
by steadfastness and by the encouragement of the scriptures we might have
hope. May the God of steadfastness and encouragement grant you to live in
harmony with one another, in accordance with Christ Jesus, so that together
you may with one voice glorify the God and Father of our Lord Jesus Christ.

Welcome one another, therefore, just as Christ has welcomed you, for the glory of God. For I tell you that Christ has become a servant of the circumcised on behalf of the truth of God in order that he might confirm the promises given to the patriarchs, and in order that the Gentiles might glorify God for his mercy. As it is written,

> 'Therefore I will confess you among the Gentiles,
> and sing praises to your name';
> and again he says,
> 'Rejoice, O Gentiles, with his people';
> and again,
> 'Praise the Lord, all you Gentiles,
> and let all the peoples praise him';
> and again Isaiah says,
> 'The root of Jesse shall come,
> the one who rises to rule the Gentiles;
> in him the Gentiles shall hope.'

May the God of hope fill you with all joy and peace in believing, so that you may abound in hope by the power of the Holy Spirit.

New Revised Standard Version

Collect

Let us pray.

Silence is kept.

Lord, we beseech thee,
give to thy people grace to hear and keep thy word
that, after the example of thy servant William Tyndale,
we may not only profess thy gospel
but also be ready to suffer and die for it,
to the honour of thy name;
through Jesus Christ our Lord.

All   Amen.

Adapted from Common Worship

Hymn: Not far beyond the sea (next page)
  or
Song: Your word is a lamp unto my feet (page 20)

Hymn: Not far beyond the sea

CORNWALL

88 6 88 6

1   Not far beyond the sea, nor high
    above the heavens, but very nigh
    your voice, O God, is heard.
    For each new step of faith we take
    you have more truth and light to break
    forth from your holy word.

2   Rooted and grounded in your love,
    with saints on earth and saints above
    we join in full accord
    to grasp the breadth, length, depth and height,
    the crucified and risen might
    of Christ, the incarnate Word.

3   Help us to press toward that mark,
    and, though our vision now is dark,
    to live by what we see;
    so, when we see you face to face,
    your truth and light our dwelling-place
    for evermore shall be.

Words: George Bradford Caird (1917–1984)
© G B Caird Memorial Trust, Mansfield College, Oxford OX1 3TF
Music: Samuel Sebastian Wesley (1810–1866)

Song: Your word is a lamp unto my feet

think I've lost— my way,_____ still you're there right be - side
love for me —_ and yet my heart for ev – er is wan-

— me: and no-thing will_ I fear as_ long as you are near._____
- dering: Je - sus, be_ my guide and hold me to_ your side. And

Please be near me to the end._____
I will love you to the end._____

Words: Amy Grant (b. 1960)
Music: Michael W Smith
Words and music © Meadowgreen Music Company/EMI Christian Music Publishing/
Universal Songs/Small Stone Media
Administered by Song Solutions Daybreak,
14 Horsted Square, Uckfield, East Sussex, TN22 1QG, UK.
info@songsolutions.org Used by permission.

III – Appointed to be Read in Churches
(by His Majesty's Special Command)

The Story: The Hampton Court Conference (1604)

Reader 1   When James I became King of England in 1603, he was petitioned by leading Puritans who wanted to express their concerns about the theology and practice of the Church of England. Early in 1604, King James convened the Hampton Court Conference – a meeting of Bishops and moderate Puritans.

Reader 2   One of the Puritans' main concerns was that people should know and understand the Bible. This led to the King commissioning a new English version and engaging leading scholars for the translation. They based their work on the Bishops' Bible of 1568, but also consulted all known earlier versions, including the work of Wycliff and Tyndale, the Rheims New Testament and the Geneva Bible. The translators began their task in 1607, and the work took them over two years, with each translator being paid 30 shillings per week.

Reader 1   The new Bible first appeared in 1611. Although it has become known as the Authorized Version, it was not officially 'authorized,' but rather simply 'appointed to be read in churches'. Perhaps more than any other book in the English language, this version of the Bible has had a far-reaching influence on Christian worship, on language and literature within the English-speaking world.

Reader 2   Much of its familiarity has been due to its place within the 1662 Book of Common Prayer. When the compilers of the 1662 Prayer Book came to revise the earlier Tudor books, one of their concerns was to update the language:

Reader 1   '....for a more perfect rendering of such portions of holy Scripture, as are inserted into the Liturgy; which, in the Epistles and Gospels especially, and in sundry other places, are now ordered to be read according to the last Translation.'

Reading: I Corinthians 14.6–12

Here beginneth the sixth verse of the fourteenth chapter of the first Epistle of St Paul to the Corinthians.

Now, brethren, if I come unto you speaking with tongues, what shall I profit you, except I shall speak to you either by revelation, or by knowledge, or by prophesying, or by doctrine? And even things without life giving sound, whether pipe or harp, except they give a distinction in the sounds, how shall it be known what is piped or harped? For if the trumpet give an uncertain sound, who shall prepare himself to the battle? So likewise ye, except ye utter by the tongue words easy to be understood, how shall it be known what is spoken? For ye shall speak into the air. There are, it may be, so many kinds of voices in the world, and none of them is without signification. Therefore if I know not the meaning of the voice, I shall be unto him that speaketh a barbarian, and he that speaketh shall be a barbarian unto me. Even so ye, forasmuch as ye are zealous of spiritual gifts, seek that ye may excel to the edifying of the church.

Authorized Version 1611

Liturgical Action

> *During the following anthem, a copy of the 1662 Book of Common Prayer is brought forward and placed centrally.*

Musical Reflection

> *Either*

And the glory of the Lord from Messiah,
by **G F Handel** (1685–1759) Page 77

> *or*

Lead me, O Lord
by **Thomas Hewitt Jones** (b. 1984) Page 89

Collect

Let us pray.

Silence is kept.

Almighty and everlasting God,
give unto us the increase of faith, hope, and charity;
and, that we may obtain that which thou dost promise,
make us to love that which thou dost command,
through Jesus Christ our Lord.
all   Amen.

Collect for the Fourteenth Sunday after Trinity,
The Book of Common Prayer 1662

Hymn: Jesus shall reign where'er the sun (turn over page)

Hymn: Jesus shall reign where'er the sun

TRURO

8 8 8 8 (L M)

1   Jesus shall reign where'er the sun
     doth his successive journeys run;
     his kingdom stretch from shore to shore,
     till moons shall wax and wane no more.

2   For him shall endless prayer be made,
     and praises throng to crown his head;
     his name like incense shall arise
     with every morning sacrifice.

3   People and realms of every tongue
     dwell on his love with sweetest song;
     and infant voices shall proclaim
     their early blessings on his name.

4   Blessings abound where'er he reigns;
     the prisoner leaps to lose his chains;
     the weary find eternal rest,
     and all the sons of want are blest.

5   Let every creature rise and bring
     peculiar honours to our King;
     angels descend with songs again,
     and earth repeat the loud amen.

Words: Isaac Watts (1674–1748)
Music: Psalmodia Evangelica 1789

IV – Into all the World

The Story: Bible Societies and Mission Organisations

Reader 1   After the restoration of the monarchy there was, at first, little
          missionary activity in the Church of England. It was assumed that
          the population was Christian and therefore not in need of
          evangelization. With the growth of the colonies, though, there came a
          growing awareness of the need to carry the Gospel to far-off lands.

Reader 2   By the early 18th century, numerous missionary societies had arisen,
          including Thomas Bray's Society for Promoting Christian Knowledge
          in 1698 and, three years later, the Society for the Propagation of the
          Gospel. The end of the century saw the foundation in 1799 of the
          Church Missionary Society by influential Anglicans including William
          Wilberforce and, five years after this, the British and Foreign Bible
          Society was born.

Reader 1   These societies saw great growth in the 19th century: some historians
          have rather cynically remarked that the missionaries to the Empire
          went forth with the crown in one hand and the Book of Common
          Prayer and the Authorized Version in the other! These stirrings of
          missionary zeal coincided with Evangelical revival in Britain. Preaching
          assumed centre stage, as Evangelical divines expounded the
          Scriptures to save souls:

Reader 2   'If, then, we have spoken the genuine unmixed word of God, and that
          only; if we have put no unnatural interpretation upon it, but [have]
          taken the known phrases in their common, obvious sense, – and
          when they were less known, explained scripture by scripture; if
          we have spoken the whole word, as occasion offered, though rather
          the parts which seemed most proper to give a check to some
          fashionable vice, or to encourage the practice of some unfashionable
          virtue; and if we have done this plainly and boldly, though with all the
          mildness and gentleness that the nature of the subject will bear; – then,
          believe ye our works, if not our words; or rather, believe them both
          together.'

John Wesley, On corrupting the word of God, Sermon 136 (ca 1728)

Liturgical Action

During the following hymn or song, the ministers move to the place of Baptism. The congregation turns to face them.

Hymn: Go forth and tell!

YANWORTH

DESCANT
5. Go forth, O__ Church of God a - rise!   Go

UNISON 1. Go forth   and tell!   O   Church of God   a - wake!   God's
TREBLES 3. Go forth   and tell   where   still the dark - ness lies;   in
UNISON 5. Go forth   and tell!   O   Church of God   a - rise!   Go

in   the   strength which__ Christ   your   Lord   sup - plies;

sav - ing news   to   all   the   na - tions take;
wealth   or want, the   sin - ner   sure - ly   dies:
in   the strength which   Christ   your   Lord   sup - plies;

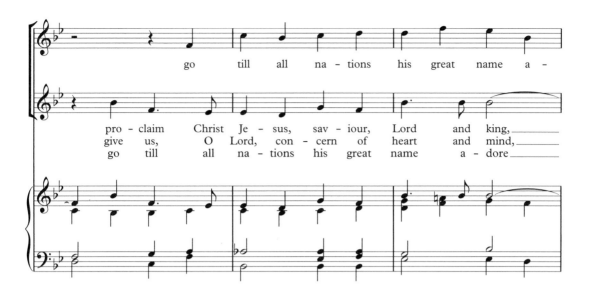

go till all na-tions his great name a-
pro-claim Christ Je-sus, sav-iour, Lord and king,
give us, O Lord, con-cern of heart and mind,
go till all na-tions his great name a - dore

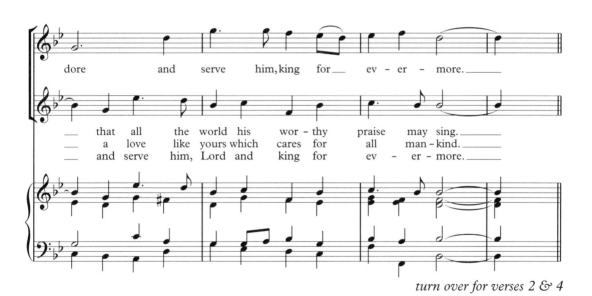

dore and serve him, king for ev-er-more.
_ that all the world his wor-thy praise may sing.
_ a love like yours which cares for all man-kind.
and serve him, Lord and king for ev - er-more.

turn over for verses 2 & 4

Words: James Seddon (1915–1983)
© Representatives of the Late James Edward Seddon/Jubilate Hymns
Music: John Barnard (b.1948)
© John Barnard/Jubilate Hymns
Words and Music administered by The Jubilate Group
4 Thorne Park Road, Chelston, Torquay, TQ2 6RX
Used with permission

or

Hymn: I, the Lord of sea and sky (page 32)

SATB

mf 2. Go forth and tell! God's love em – bra – ces all; he
mf 4. Go forth and tell! The doors are o – pen wide: share

mf 2. Go forth____ and tell! God's love em – bra – ces all; he
mf 4. Go forth____ and tell! The_ doors are o –pen wide: share

mf 2. Go forth and tell!____ God's love em – bra –ces all; he
mf 4. Go forth and tell!____ The doors are o –pen wide: share

mf 2. Go forth and tell!____ God's love em – bra –ces all;____ he
mf 4. Go forth and tell!____ The doors are o –pen wide:____ share

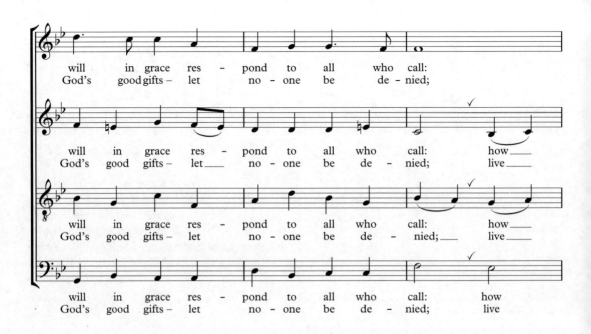

will in grace res – pond to all who call:
God's good gifts – let no – one be de – nied;

will in grace res – pond to all who call: how____
God's good gifts – let____ no – one be de – nied; live____

will in grace res – pond to all who call: how____
God's good gifts – let no – one be de – nied;___ live____

will in grace res – pond to all who call: how
God's good gifts – let no – one be de – nied; live

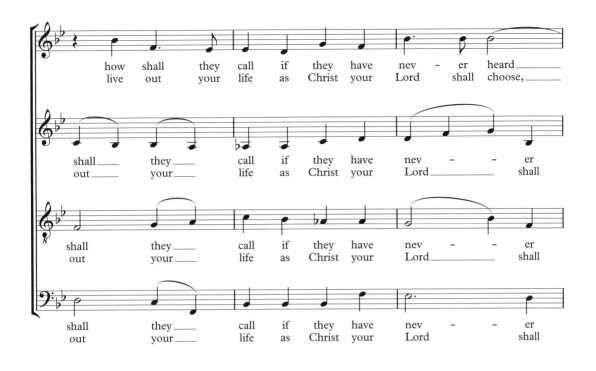

how   shall   they   call   if   they   have   nev – er   heard
live   out   your   life   as   Christ   your   Lord   shall   choose,

shall   they   call   if   they   have   nev – – er
out   your   life   as   Christ   your   Lord   shall

shall   they   call   if   they   have   nev – – er
out   your   life   as   Christ   your   Lord   shall

shall   they   call   if   they   have   nev – – er
out   your   life   as   Christ   your   Lord   shall

the   gra – cious   in – vi – ta – tion   of   his   word?
your   ran – somed   powers   for   his   sole   glo – ry   use.

heard   the   gra – cious   in – vi – ta – tion   of   his   word?
choose, your   ran – somed   powers   for   his   sole   glo – ry   use.

heard the   gra – cious   in – vi – ta – tion   of   his   word?
choose, your   ran – somed   powers   for   his   sole   glo – ry   use.

heard the   gra – cious   in – vi – ta – tion   of   his   word?
choose, your   ran – somed   powers   for   his   sole   glo – ry   use.

Hymn: I, the Lord of sea and sky

1. *mf* I, the Lord   of sea   and sky,   I have heard   my
2. *mp* I, the Lord   of snow   and rain,   I have borne   my
3. *f* I, the Lord   of wind   and flame,   I will tend   the

v1 SOPRANO
v2 TENOR and BASS
v3 ALL

peo - ple   cry.   All who dwell   in dark   and sin
peo - ple's pain.   I have wept   for love   of them.
poor and   lame.   I will set   a feast   for them.

after verse 3 go to ⊕

Words: based on Isaiah 6
Music: Daniel Schutte SJ (b.1947) arranged by Malcolm Archer (b.1952)
Words and music © 1981, OCP. Published by OCP Publications
5536 NE Hassalo, Portland, OR 97213, USA

The Gospel reading is read from the place of baptism

Gospel Reading: Matthew 28.18–20

The holy Gospel is written in the twenty-eighth chapter of the Gospel according to Matthew, beginning at the eighteenth verse.

All   **Glory be to thee, O Lord.**

And Jesus came and spake unto them, saying, All power is given unto me in heaven and in earth. Go ye therefore, and teach all nations, baptizing them in the name of the Father, and of the Son, and of the Holy Ghost: teaching them to observe all things whatsoever I have commanded you: and, lo, I am with you always, even unto the end of the world. Amen.

This is the Gospel of the Lord.

All   **Praise be to thee, O Christ.**

Thanksgiving for Baptism

A minister leads the following Thanksgiving for Baptism.

Water is poured into the Font.

God in Christ gives us water welling up for eternal life.
With joy you will draw water from the wells of salvation.

All   **Lord, give us this water and we shall thirst no more.**

Let us give thanks to the Lord our God.

All   **It is right to give thanks and praise.**

Blessed are you, sovereign God of all,
to you be glory and praise for ever.
You are our light and our salvation.
From the deep waters of death
you have raised your Son to life in triumph.
Grant that all who have been born anew by water and the Spirit
may daily be renewed in your image,
walk by the light of faith,
and serve you in newness of life;
through your anointed Son, Jesus Christ,
to whom with you and the Holy Spirit
we lift our voices of praise.
Blessed be God, Father, Son and Holy Spirit.

All   **Blessed be God for ever.**

Thanksgiving for Baptism, Common Worship: Daily Prayer

Musical Reflection

Either

How lovely are the messengers
by **Felix Mendelssohn** (1809–1847) Page 97

or

Vox Christi
by **Philip Wilby** (b.1949) Page 107

or

Taizé Chant: In the Lord I'll be ever thankful (see below)

Taizé Chant: In the Lord I'll be ever thankful

please turn over for verses 3, 4 & 5

3. I call up-on the Lord God who is wor-thy of

4. My soul shall sing to you;

5. With joy you will draw wa - ter at the foun - tain of sal -

OSTINATO
Dm C F   F/A   B♭   C   Dm C F   F/A

In the Lord I'll be ev - er thank - ful, in the Lord I will re -

praise.

you have done won - drous things, O God.

-va - tion.   Give thanks to the

C   B♭   A   Dm   C

-joice!   Look to God, do not be a - fraid. Lift up your

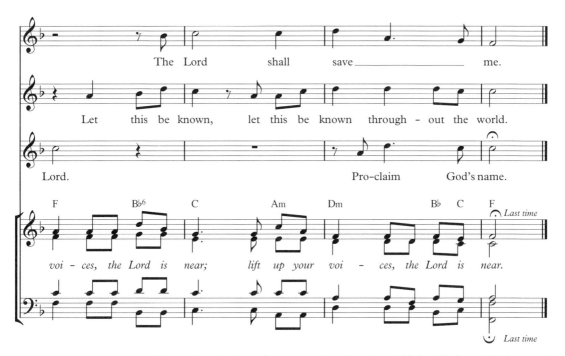

The Lord shall save me.

Let this be known, let this be known through-out the world.

Lord. Pro-claim God's name.

voi - ces, the Lord is near; lift up your voi - ces, the Lord is near.

Words from the Taizé Community based on Isaiah 12.2–6 (A Song of Deliverance)
and Psalm 18.2–3
Music: Jacques Berthier (1923–1994)
Words and music © 1998 Ateliers et Presses de Taizé, 71250 Taizé, France

Collect

Let us pray for the extension of Christ's Kingdom throughout the world.

Silence is kept.

How beautiful are the feet of them that preach the gospel of peace;
and bring glad tidings of good things.

O God, our heavenly Father,
who didst manifest thy love by sending thine only-begotten Son into the world
that all might live through him:
Pour thy Spirit upon thy Church
that it may fulfil his command to preach the Gospel to every creature;
send forth, we beseech thee, labourers into thy harvest;
defend them in all dangers and temptations;
and hasten the time when the fulness of the Gentiles shall be gathered in,
and all Israel shall be saved;
through the same thy Son Jesus Christ our Lord. Amen.

Occasional Prayers, The Prayer Book as Proposed in 1928

Hymn: Thou whose almighty word

MOSCOW

66 4 66 64

1   Thou whose almighty word
     chaos and darkness heard,
         and took their flight;
     hear us, we humbly pray,
     and where the Gospel-day
     sheds not its glorious ray,
         let there be light.

2   Thou, who didst come to bring
     on thy redeeming wing
         healing and sight,
     health to the sick in mind,
     sight to the inly blind,
     O now to all mankind
         let there be light.

3   Spirit of truth and love,
     life-giving, holy Dove,
         speed forth thy flight;
     move on the water's face,
     bearing the lamp of grace,
     and in earth's darkest place
         let there be light.

4   Holy and blessed Three,
     glorious Trinity,
         Wisdom, Love, Might;
     boundless as ocean's tide
     rolling in fullest pride,
     through the earth far and wide
         let there be light.

Words: John Marriott (1780–1825) and Thomas Raffles (1788–1863)
Music: Felice de Giardini (1716–1796)

During this hymn, the ministers return from the Font.

They may sprinkle the congregation with water from the Font.

These words may be used

Remember your baptism into Christ.

All   Thanks be to God.

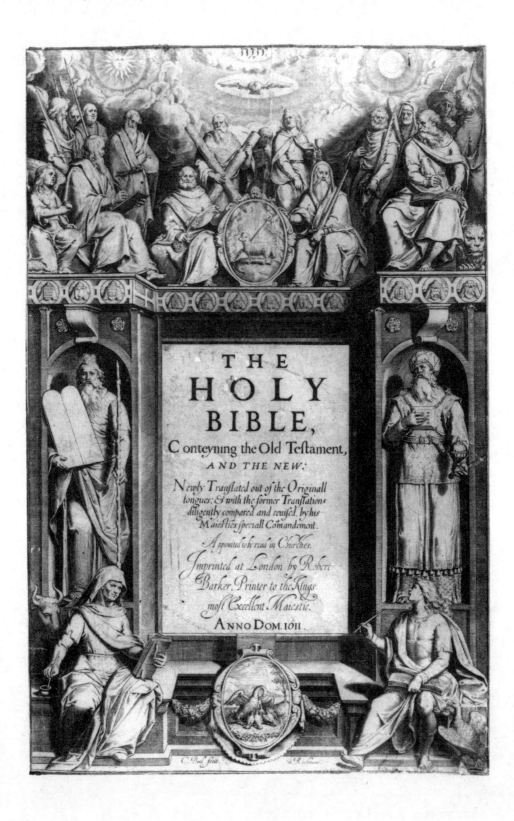

V – According to the Latest Translation

The story: The Bible in the Twentieth Century

Reader 1   The past 130 years have seen many translations and paraphrases of the Bible. Beginning with the Revised Version of 1881, some have kept a deliberate echo of the King James version: the Revised Standard Version of 1952 and the New Revised Standard Version of 1989. Other popular versions have included the New English Bible – which, like the Authorized Version, was compiled in the Jerusalem Chamber at Westminster Abbey – and its successor, the Revised English Bible, the Jerusalem Bible and the New International Version.

Reader 2   While these versions tried to render faithfully the original Hebrew and Greek texts in modern English, others have adopted a freer approach. J B Phillips' The Bible in Modern English was compiled specifically for use in schools. The Good News Bible aimed to present the Bible's message 'in a standard, everyday, natural English.' Some versions have been written in regional dialect. And recently, the Street Bible and Eugene Petersen's The Message have become popular examples of Biblical paraphrase, both of them attempt to bridge 'two language worlds, the world of the Bible and the world of today.'

Reader 1   The linguistic impact of the King James Bible is such that much of the language has persisted to the present day and many phrases are still commonplace. This story uses just a few of them, [highlighted in italics]. Most are lifted directly from the 1611 King James Version.

Reading: 'Sarah's Dinner'

Sarah decided to give a dinner party for family and friends, and she sent out many invitations – *three score and ten* to be precise. Her husband, Jack, was worried. 'It'll cost us a fortune,' he said. Sarah replied, 'Well, *it's better to give than to receive*. So *let us eat, drink and be merry* while we're about it. Anyway, *as you sow, so shall you reap!*'

Jack protested, '*Man does not live by bread alone.* Besides, why invite Great Uncle Tom – he's *as old as the hills* and *at his wits' end*. He'll barely make it *by the skin of his teeth* – if he's got any left! And as for that wayward brother of mine – talk about *a man after his own heart*. Can't see why we should waste good money on <u>him</u>. *Am I my brother's keeper?*'

'Oh come on, Jack', retorted Sarah, 'that's just *sour grapes*.'

'No it's not. He was always his father's favourite, *the apple of his eye*, until his *fall from grace*. Shows what happens when you *spare the rod and spoil the child*. Ha! *How are the mighty fallen. Can a leopard change his spots?* Not him – and feeding him would be casting *pearls before swine!*'

'Sorry, Jack', said Sarah, 'but it's time to stop this *eye for an eye, tooth for a tooth* attitude. *Blessed are the peacemakers. For everything there is a time and a season,* and I for one think it's time to be reconciled. After all, *love covers a multitude of sins* and he is your own *flesh and blood*. I know he's been a *thorn in the flesh* at times, but that doesn't give us the right to *cast the first stone*. Besides, these days he might be the *salt of the earth*.'

Jack realised that he wouldn't win an argument with Sarah until the day he *gave up the ghost*. So he changed the subject back to the food: 'So how are we going to cater for this lot? That's *the root of the matter*.'

Sarah replied, 'Yes, that is a bit of a *fly in the ointment*. But we could do a casserole – there's a chicken in the freezer.'

'A chicken? One chicken? I know *a bird in the hand is worth two in the bush*, if all these folk turn up we'll need to lead a whole *lamb to the slaughter*. Besides, last time you did a chicken casserole, it was literally a *baptism of fire* – came out of the oven as a *burnt offering*. Talk about *ashes to ashes, dust to dust!*'

'In which case,' snapped Sarah, 'you can enjoy watching your brother *bite the dust!*'

'Oh, very funny!' said Jack. 'What about drink?'

'No problem – there's plenty of gin and tonic to go round for starters, a case of wine in the cellar, and a large bottle of malt for afters.'

'So then', said Jack, 'to sum up, the booze is great but there's only one measly chicken. I see what they mean when they say *the spirit is willing but the flesh is weak*.'

And Sarah laughed.

Alternative Reading: Matthew 13.1,3–9, 18–23, 34–35

A reading from the Gospel according to Matthew.

Jesus addressed his congregation, telling stories.

'What do you make of this? A farmer planted seed. As he scattered the seed, some of it fell on the road, and birds ate it. Some fell in the gravel; it sprouted quickly but didn't put down roots, so when the sun came up it withered just as quickly. Some fell in the weeds; as it came up, it was strangled by the weeds. Some fell on good earth, and produced a harvest beyond his wildest dreams.

'Are you listening to this? Really listening?'

'Study this story of the farmer planting seed. When anyone hears news of the kingdom and doesn't take it in, it just remains on the surface, and so the Evil One comes along and plucks it right out of that person's heart. This is the seed the farmer scatters on the road.

'The seed cast in the gravel – this is the person who hears and instantly responds with enthusiasm. But there is no soil of character, and so when the emotions wear off and some difficulty arrives, there is nothing to show for it.

'The seed cast in the weeds is the person who hears the kingdom news, but weeds of worry and illusions about getting more and wanting everything under the sun strangle what was heard, and nothing comes of it.

'The seed cast on good earth is the person who hears and takes in the News, and then produced a harvest beyond his wildest dreams.'

All Jesus did that day was tell stories – a long storytelling afternoon.

His storytelling fulfilled the prophecy:

I will open my mouth and tell stories;
I will bring out into the open
things hidden since the world's first day

Your word, O Lord, is a lantern to our feet
All   and a light upon our path.

Hymn: God in his wisdom (below)
   or
Song: Speak, O Lord (page 50)

Hymn: God in his wisdom

FRAGRANCE

98 98 98

1   God in his wisdom, for our learning
        gave his inspired and holy word:
    promise of Christ, for our discerning,
        by which our souls are moved and stirred,
    finding our hearts within us burning
        when, as of old, his voice is heard.

2   Symbol and story, song and saying,
        life-bearing truths for heart and mind,
    God in his sovereign grace displaying
        tenderest care for humankind,
    Jesus our Lord this love portraying,
        open our eyes to seek and find.

3   Come then with prayer and contemplation,
        see how in Scripture Christ is known;
    wonder anew at such salvation
        here in these sacred pages shown;
    lift every heart in adoration,
        children of God by grace alone!

Song: Speak, O Lord

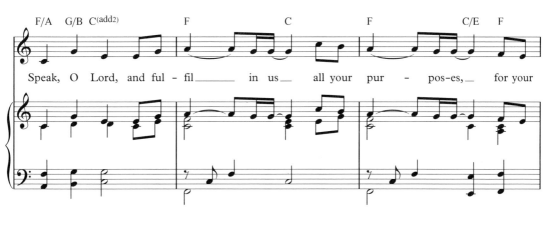

Speak, O Lord, and ful-fil_____ in us__ all your pur - pos-es, __ for your

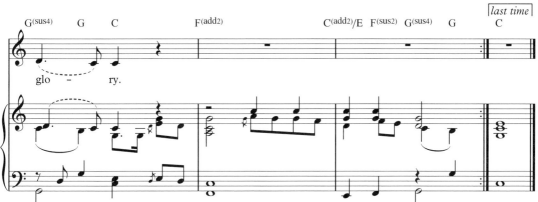

glo - ry.

2   Teach us, Lord, full obedience,
     holy reverence, true humility.
     Test our thoughts and our attitudes
     in the radiance of your purity.
     Cause our faith to rise, cause our eyes to see
     your majestic love and authority.
     Words of power that can never fail;
     let their truth prevail over unbelief.

3   Speak, O Lord, and renew our minds;
     help us grasp the heights of your plans for us.
     Truths unchanged from the dawn of time
     that will echo down through eternity.
     And by grace we'll stand on your promises,
     and by faith we'll walk as you walk with us.
     Speak, O Lord, till your church is built
     and the earth is filled with your glory.

Words and music: Keith Getty (b.1974) and Stuart Townend (b.1963)
Words and music © 2005 Thankyou Music
Administered (UK and Europe) by Kingswaysongs.com <tym@kingsway.co.uk>
Remaining territories administered by worshiptogether.com songs
Used by permission.

Collect

Let us pray.

Silence is kept.

Merciful God,
teach us to be faithful in change and uncertainty,
that trusting in your word
and obeying your will
we may enter the unfailing joy of Jesus Christ our Lord.

All   Amen.

Additional Collect for the Last Sunday after Trinity,
Common Worship

¶ The Sending Out

Commissioning

Will you continue in the apostles' teaching and fellowship,
in the breaking of the bread, and in the prayers?

All **With the help of God, I will.**

Will you persevere in resisting evil,
and, whenever you fall into sin, repent and return to the Lord?

All **With the help of God, I will.**

Will you proclaim by word and example
the good news of God in Christ?

All **With the help of God, I will.**

Will you seek and serve Christ in all people,
loving your neighbour as yourself?

All **With the help of God, I will.**

Will you acknowledge Christ's authority over human society,
by prayer for the world and its leaders,
by defending the weak, and by seeking peace and justice?

All **With the help of God, I will.**

The Lord's Prayer

So let us pray that God's word may be fulfilled
in the words our Saviour taught us.

All **Our Father, who art in heaven,**
hallowed be thy name;
thy kingdom come;
thy will be done;
on earth as it is in heaven.
Give us this day our daily bread.
And forgive us our trespasses,
as we forgive those who trespass against us.
And lead us not into temptation;
but deliver us from evil.
For thine is the kingdom,
the power and the glory,
for ever and ever.
Amen.

1   You shall go out with joy
     and come again in peace;
     the mountains and the hills
     shall sing and never cease;
        the Son of God is ris'n again,
        his love has conquered death's domain.

2   The trees in every field
     shall clap their hands, and say
     'Come shout aloud, and help
     us celebrate this day!'
        Jesus, the King, has burst the grave,
        and lives once more to heal and save.

3   The Word, like rain or snow,
     has come down from above,
     and now reveals to all
     God's purposes of love;
        the Word made flesh, once dead, now lives,
        new life to all he freely gives.

4   The myrtle for the briar,
     the cypress for the thorn,
     shall rise to tell the world
     of its awaking dawn.
        Jesus, the Life, the Truth, the Way,
        has ushered in God's great new day.

for last verse descant, please turn over

Words: Tom Wright (b. 1948) based on Isaiah 55.10–13
Copyright © The Right Reverend N T Wright
Music: Paul Spicer (b. 1952) from 'Easter Oratorio'
© 2000 Paul Spicer. Used with permission.

The Myr – tle for__ the__ briar, the   cy-press for the__ thorn,   shall

rise to tell the   world that__ this new   day_____ was born.

Je – sus the__ Truth,   has u – shered in__ God's great   new   day.

Blessing

The Father, whose glory fills the heavens,
cleanse you by his holiness
and send you to proclaim his word.

All   **Amen.**

Christ, the Word made flesh
fill you with his grace and truth
that you may behold his glory.

All   **Amen.**

The Spirit of truth
lead you into all truth,
and strengthen you to proclaim the word and works of God.

All   **Amen.**

And the blessing of God
the Father, the Son and the Holy Spirit,
be among you and remain with you always.

All   **Amen.**

Dismissal

Hear the teaching of Jesus:
'Blessed are those who hear the word of God and obey it.'
Go now to do God's will.

All   **Thanks be to God.**

the Word Revealed

PART II: CHORAL RESOURCES

Anthem: O Praise the Lord

Words: Psalm 117. 1–2

Music: Adrian Batten (c.1591–1637)

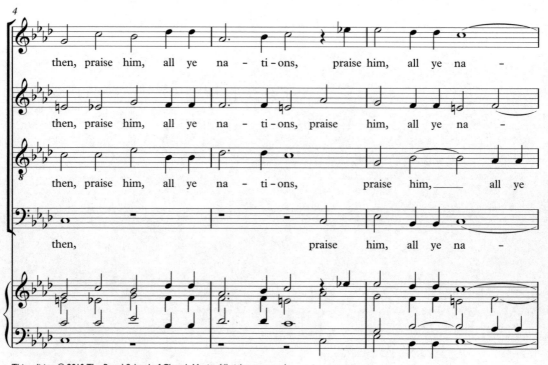

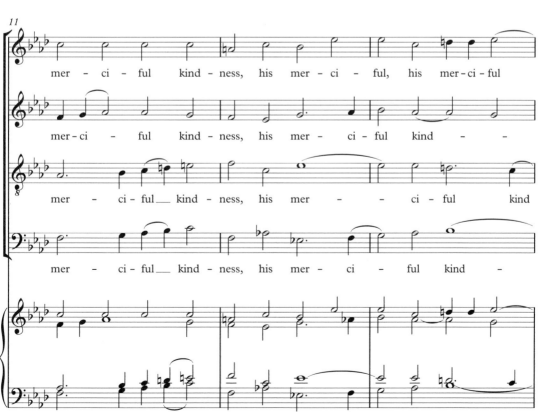

kind - ness is ev - er - more and more to - wards
— ness is ev - er - more and more to - wards
— ness is ev - er - more and more to - wards
— ness is ev - er - more and more to - wards

us. And the truth____ of the Lord, and the truth of the
us. And the truth____ of the Lord, and the truth of the
us. And the truth____ of the Lord, and the truth of the
us. And the truth____ of the Lord, and the truth of the

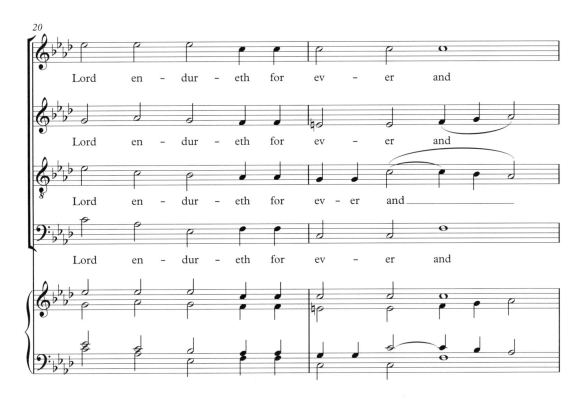

Go back to page 9

Anthem: Teach me, O Lord

Words: Psalm 119. 33

Music: Thomas Attwood (1765–1838)
edited Anthony Greening

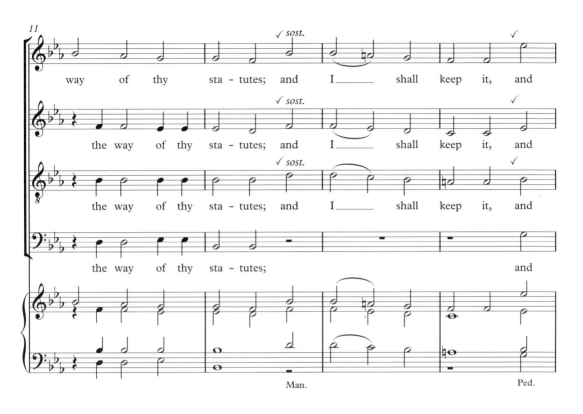

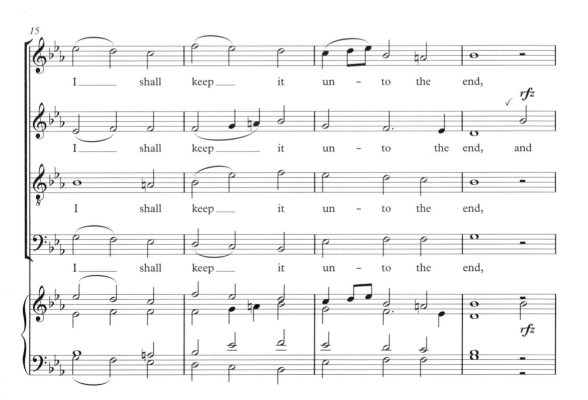

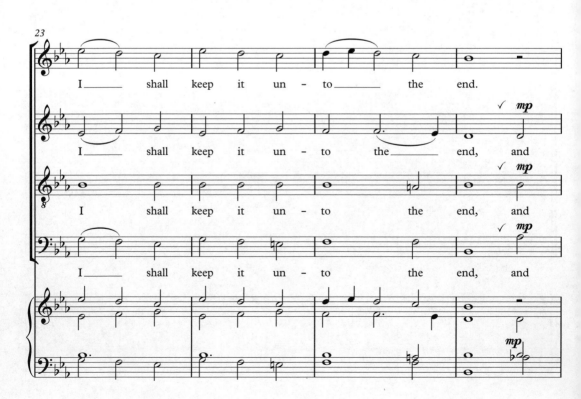

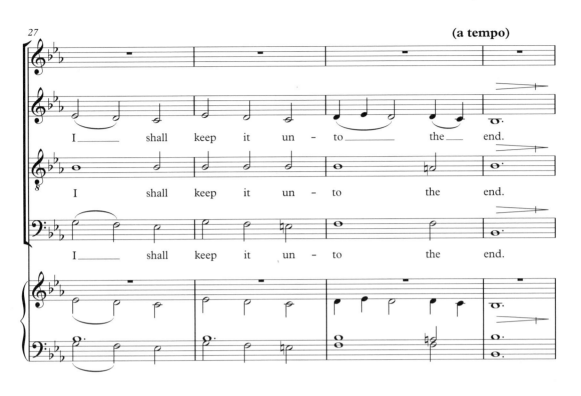

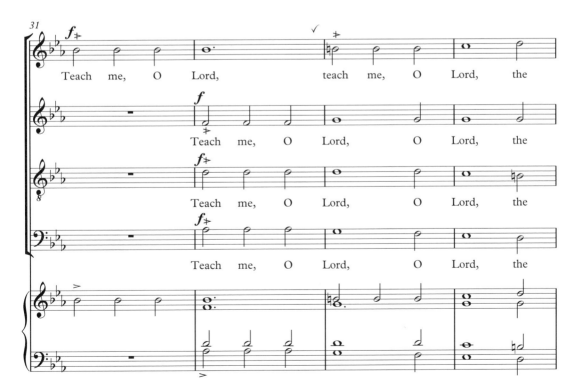

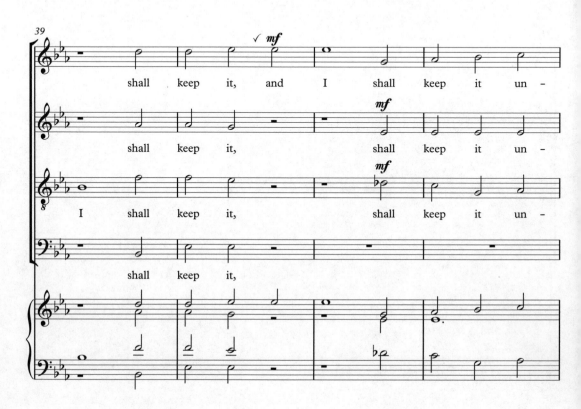

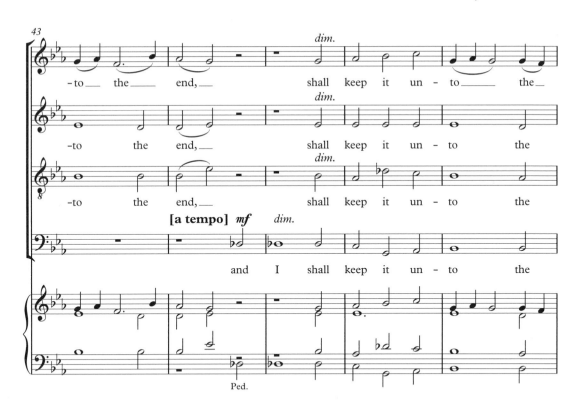

Go back to page 9

Anthem: Teach us, good Lord

Words: St Ignatius of Loyola

Music: David Ogden (b. 1966)

Smooth and sustained ♩ = 56

mp

Teach us, good Lord, to serve thee _____ as thou de-serv-est; _____ to give and not to count the cost; _____ to fight and not to heed the

wounds;_____ to toil and not to seek for rest;_____

__ to la - bour and to ask for no re - ward,_____ save that of

know - ing that we do thy will;_____ save that of know - ing

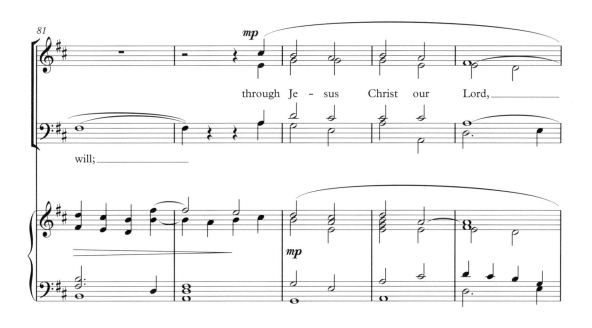

through Je - sus Christ our Lord,_____

will;_____

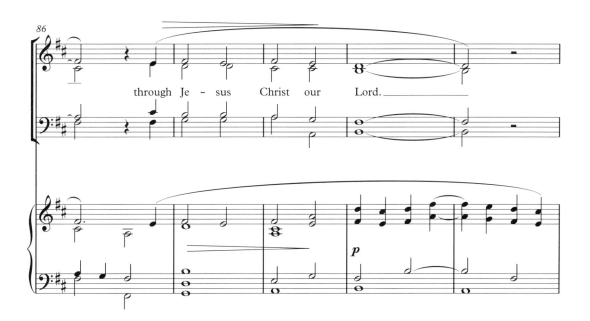

through Je - sus Christ our Lord._____

Go back to page 9

Anthem: And the glory of the Lord
from Messiah

Words: Isaiah 40.5

Music: George Frederic Handel (1685–1759)
edited by David Iliff

And the glo - ry, the glo-ry of the Lord,

glo-ry of the Lord,   the glo-ry of the Lord,

And the glo - ry, the glo-ry of the Lord shall be re -

And the glo - ry, the glo-ry of the Lord,

shall be re - veal - ed,

-veal - ed,   and the glo - ry, the glo-ry of the

shall be re - veal - ed,   shall be re -

re - veal - ed,

re - veal - ed,

re - veal - ed,

re - veal - ed,

and all flesh___ shall see___ it to - ge - ther,

and all flesh___ shall

see__ it to - ge-ther, the mouth of the Lord hath

it to - ge-ther, and the glo - ry, the glo-ry of the

see it to - ge - ther,

see__ it to - ge - ther,

spo - ken it,

Lord, shall be re - veal - ed, and all

and all flesh__

and all flesh__

and the glo-ry, the glo-ry, the glo-ry of the

shall see it to-ge-ther,

flesh___ shall see_ it to ge-ther,

and all flesh___ shall see_ it to ge-ther,

Lord shall be re - veal - ed,

and the glo-ry, the glo-ry of the Lord shall be re - veal -

and the glo-ry, the glo-ry of the Lord

and the glo-ry, the glo-ry of the Lord shall be re -

hath spo - ken it, for the mouth   of   the

hath spo - ken it, for the mouth   of   the

hath spo - ken it,   for the mouth of the Lord,___ the

hath spo - ken it,   for the mouth of the Lord,___ the

Adagio

Lord_____   hath spo - ken it.

Lord_____   hath spo - ken it.

mouth of the Lord___   hath spo - ken it.

mouth of the Lord___   hath spo - ken it.

Adagio

Go back to page 25

Anthem: Lead me, O Lord

Words: Psalms 5. 8 (King James Version)   Music: Thomas Hewitt Jones (b. 1984)

Lead me, O Lord, in thy right-eous-ness

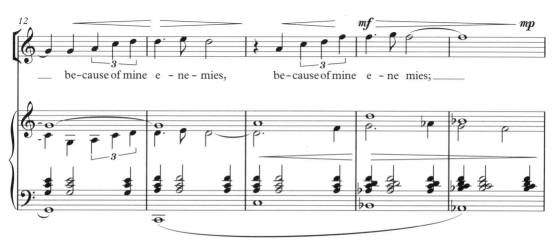

be-cause of mine e - ne - mies, be-cause of mine e - ne mies;

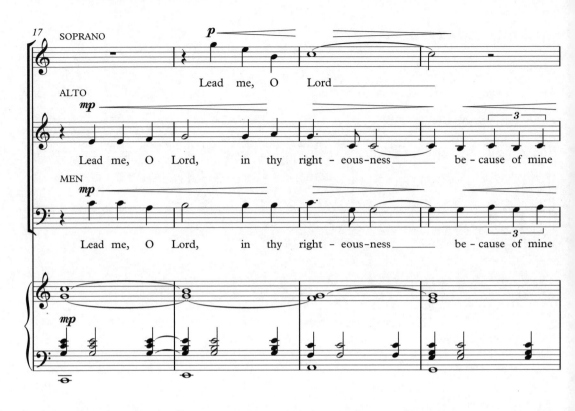

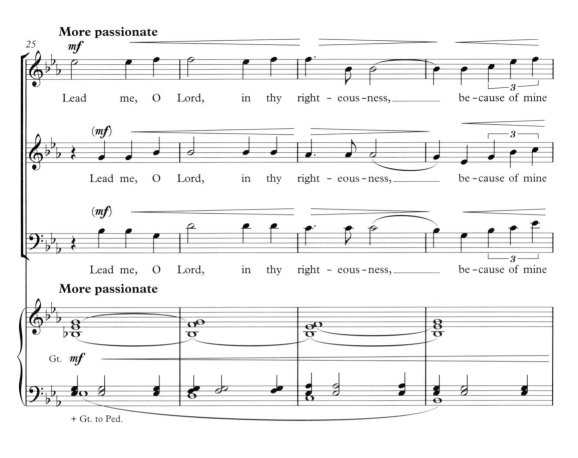

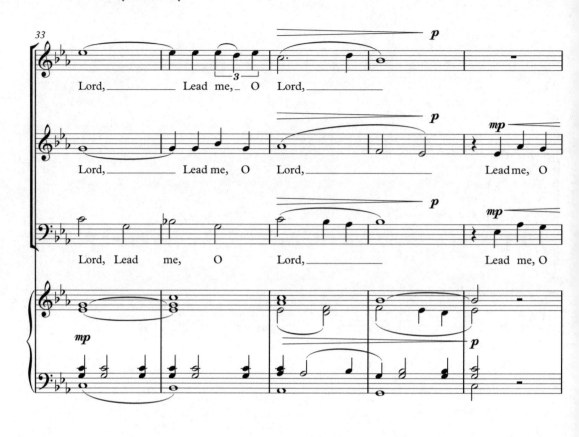

Passionate

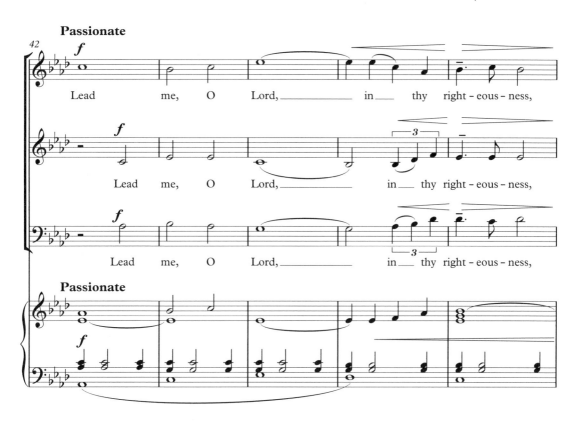

Broadly

Hopeful

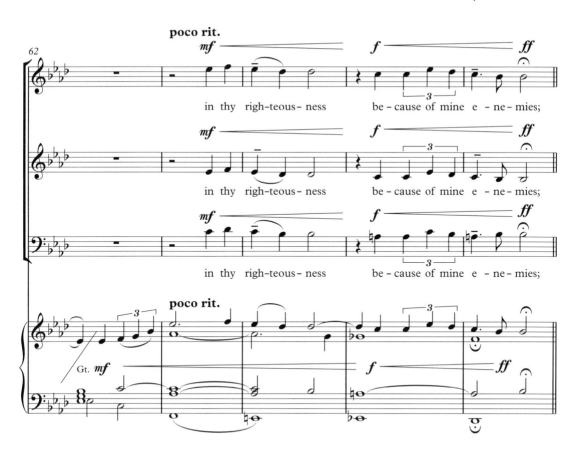

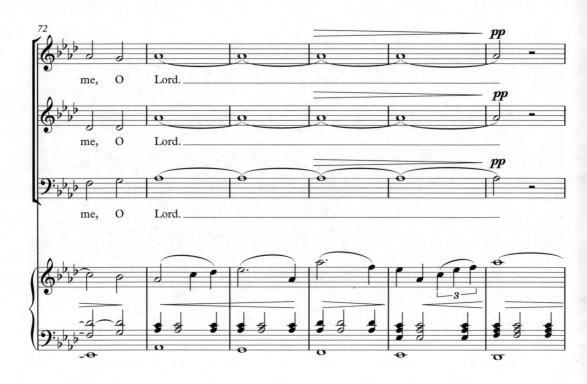

Go back to page 25

Anthem: How lovely are the messengers
from St Paul

Words: from Romans 10. 15, 18   Music: Felix Mendelssohn (1809–1847)

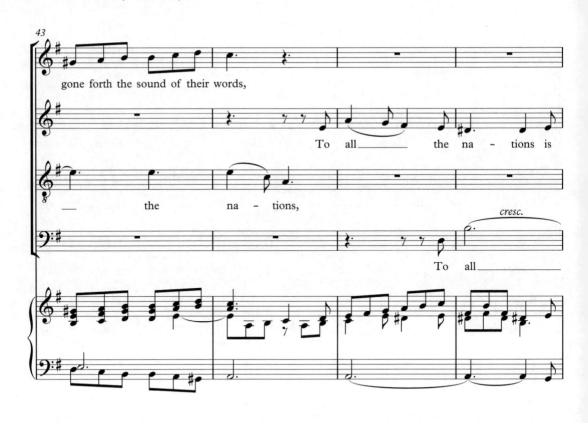

preach us the gos - pel of peace.

preach us the gos - pel of peace.

preach us the gos - pel of peace.

peace,___ the gos - pel of peace.

Go back to page 41

Anthem: Vox Christi

Words: from 'The Great Commission'
Matthew 28. 18–20

Music: Philip Wilby (b.1949)

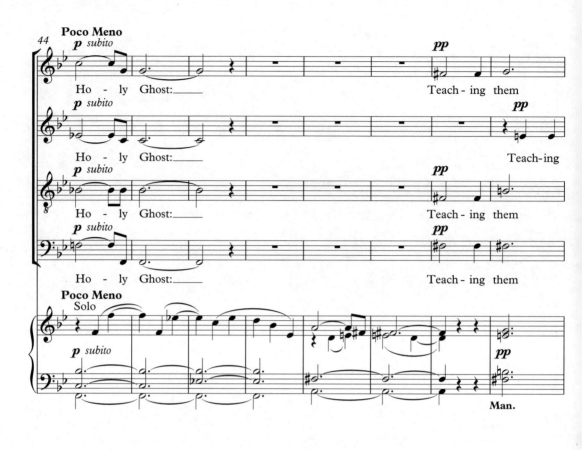

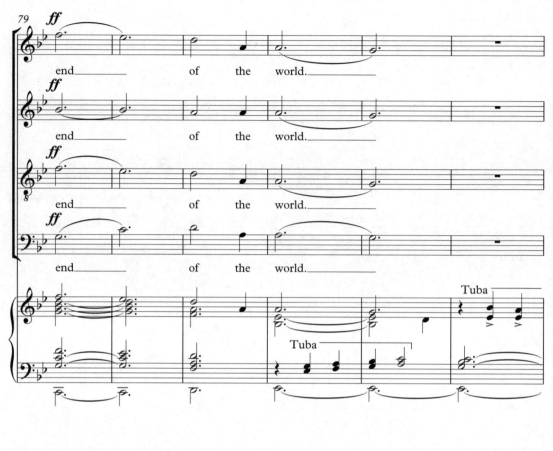

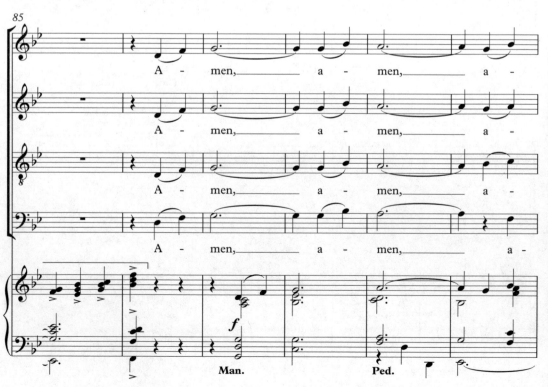

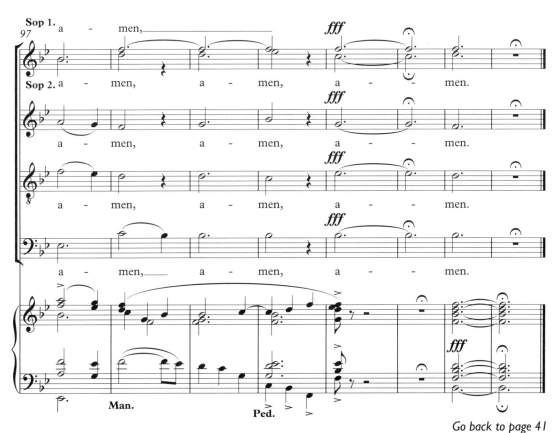

Go back to page 41

Hymn: You shall go out with joy

CHRISTCHURCH

1   You shall go out with joy
     and come again in peace;
     the mountains and the hills
     shall sing and never cease;
        the Son of God is ris'n again,
        his love has conquered death's domain.

2   The trees in every field
     shall clap their hands, and say
     'Come shout aloud, and help
     us celebrate this day!'
        Jesus, the King, has burst the grave,
        and lives once more to heal and save.

3   The Word, like rain or snow,
     has come down from above,
     and now reveals to all
     God's purposes of love;
        the Word made flesh, once dead, now lives,
        new life to all he freely gives.

4   The myrtle for the briar,
     the cypress for the thorn,
     shall rise to tell the world
     of its awaking dawn.
        Jesus, the Life, the Truth, the Way,
        has ushered in God's great new day.

Words: Tom Wright (b. 1948)
based on Isaiah 55.10–13
Copyright © The Right Reverend N T Wright
Music: Charles Steggall (1826–1905)

Go back to page 57